Blue Ridge Harvest

A Region's  in Photogra[

An essay from the Blue Ridge Parkway
Folklife Project conducted by the American
Folklife Center in cooperation with the
National Park Service in August and
September 1978

Edited by Lyntha Scott Eiler, Terry Eiler,
and Carl Fleischhauer

Library of Congress
Washington
1981

Cover: Veoma Easter peels and cores apples for slicing and drying, Surry County, North Carolina.

Title page: Foxhounds, Carroll County, Virginia

Publications of the American Folklife Center; No. 7

Library of Congress Cataloging in Publication Data

Main entry under title:

Blue Ridge harvest.

    Supt. of Docs. no.: LC 1.2:B62

      1. Blue Ridge Mountains—Social life and customs —Pictorial works. 2. Folk-lore—Blue Ridge Mountains—Pictorial works. 3. Blue Ridge Mountains—Description and travel—Views. I. Eiler, Lyntha Scott. II. Eiler, Terry. III. Fleischhauer, Carl. IV. Blue Ridge Parkway Folklife Project. V. American Folklife Center. VI. United States. National Park Service.

F217.B6B58   975.5   80–607940

ISBN 0–8444–0341–5

Contents

**The Blue Ridge Parkway,
Alleghany County,
North Carolina**

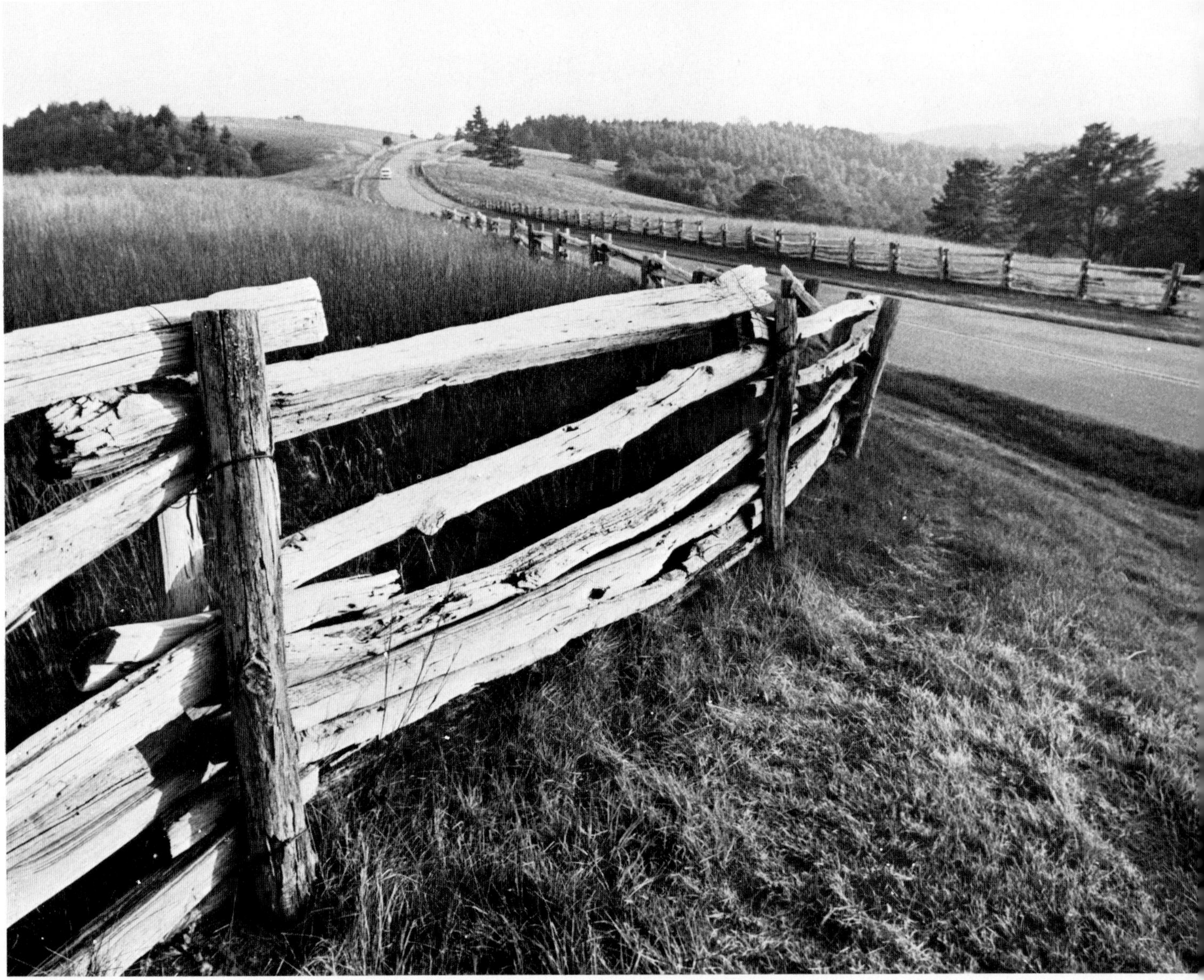

Introduction

The central Blue Ridge is a varied and dynamic region, deeply traditional and simultaneously modern, where customary expression has evolved by selective choice. The region's agriculture ranges from the relatively antique tools and techniques used to grow, harvest, and cure tobacco to the newer methods—and the use of migrant labor—employed to grow and harvest the newer cash crop of cabbage. A small hamlet is still a "community," but other communities of interest or geography affect the lives of people who live along the ridge. Some Blue Ridge citizens, like Janet and D.J. Keith, are conscious of the region's heritage and teach it in school. For others, like Carrie Severt and McKinley Brim, tradition manifests itself in the activities of daily life.

Folklife sometimes seems far away and quaint, covered by a patina of history, but these photographs are intended to dispel this impression and convey the "presentness" of folklife. An activity like foxhunting in the mountains may seem like a pioneer affair, but our pictures show not only a pack of hounds running for the pleasure of two present-day Virginians, but also a scene from a regional hunt which drew men from all over the upper South. A photograph of an immersion baptism is not a document from the Depression but a contemporary scene of the link between God, man, and nature.

Life in the Blue Ridge is richly complex and cannot be described as simple or culturally uniform. There are no "pure folk communities" here—or, for that matter, anywhere else in the United States. The lives of the people we met and talked with are similar in many ways to the lives of many others in our complex society. Like us, the people of the Blue Ridge live in a world of cultural options, social networks, and diverse traditions and experiences.

This book is one product of the Blue Ridge Parkway Folklife Project, conducted in 1978 by the American Folklife Center in cooperation with the National Park Service. The Park Service, well-known as the custodian of America's most striking natural sites, has also been for many years a custodian and interpreter of our nation's culture and history. It was therefore not surprising that the Park Service and the American Folklife Center should cooperate to conduct a folk cultural project, in accordance with the center's mandate to work with other government agencies. Together we selected the Blue Ridge Parkway as the site for a field research project.

The parkway's 469 miles cover more territory than a small team of cultural specialists could investigate during the course of a summer project. Since much of the route emphasizes natural rather than cultural scenes, the project area was limited to a region along about a hundred-mile stretch where neighboring farms, communities, and churches readily meet the eye—portions of seven counties along the parkway between Rocky Knob in Virginia and Doughton Park in North Carolina.

2

Our goal for the project was to mount an intensive field survey of the folk cultural traditions along both sides of the Blue Ridge today. The team talked with hundreds of people—with many of them at length. We made hundreds of tape recordings—of conversations, story-telling, family histories, descriptions of processes like cooking, canning, and sawmilling, musical performances, church services, and fox hunts—and took thousands of photographs—of houses, people, crops, home interiors, baptisms, and dances.

The team consisted of folklorists Charles K. Wolfe, Middle Tennessee State University, who served as field coordinator; Thomas A. Adler, Indiana University; Geraldine Johnson, Strayer College; Patrick Mullen, Ohio State University; Blanton Owen, Ferrum College; Margaret Owen, Ferrum College; and photographers Lyntha Scott Eiler and Terry Eiler, Ohio University. Center staff members Carl Fleischhauer and Howard W. Marshall joined in the work, as did five Park Service employees who assisted with the fieldwork as special interns and gained insights into traditional life to aid them in their regular work: Harley Jolley, Wes Leishman, Richard McCamant, George Price, Jr., and Arnold Schofield.

Wally Macnow of the Department of the Interior helped organize the project and participated in the fieldwork. Gary Everhardt, superintendent of the Blue Ridge Parkway and former American Folklife Center board member, lent his sympathetic support, and Andrew Kardos of the parkway professional staff helped the effort in many ways. The entire project could never have taken shape without the backing of William Whalen, director of the National Park Service and member of the Folklife Center's board, and Vernon Dame, the National Park Service's director of interpretation and visitor services.

This book, then, is one of the products of the Blue Ridge Parkway Folklife Project. Although everyone involved in the effort hopes it will appeal to readers across the nation, we particularly hope it will find a warm reception from the people it celebrates—the residents of the central Blue Ridge. To them we dedicate this book and offer our deepest gratitude for permitting us to document their lives and to share its richness with others.

Alan Jabbour
Director, American Folklife Center

**Transporting cabbages
on Road 608, Patrick
County, Virginia**

Cultural
Landscape

Hayfields along Road
804, Floyd County,
Virginia

Road 1422 and the
Blue Ridge, Alleghany
County, North Carolina

The Region

For most of the 469-mile drive along the Blue Ridge Parkway, woodlands alternate with prospects of broad valleys and distant mountains. But if nature lays first claim to our eyes, the traditional culture of the people is also visible, particularly along one stretch of the parkway spanning southwestern Virginia and northwestern North Carolina. Here the parkway traveler sees the complex interweaving of nature and culture which gives the region its character.

Driving southwest from Roanoke, one climbs Bent Mountain and, beyond its summit, encounters a broad, high plateau stretching away from the Blue Ridge to the southwest. The first county along the plateau, Floyd, offers views of green valleys, woodsy knolls, and small farms and rural settlements. Looking east from the other side of the parkway, one sees the piedmont valleys of Franklin County. The creeks flow away from the Blue Ridge on either side, those on the left toward the Atlantic Ocean and those on the right to the Gulf of Mexico.

The dominant Anglo-American culture of this region shares traditions with a larger area that runs north into Pennsylvania and east into the southern piedmont. Also distinguishable are strands of German-American life—an anglicized German name on a mailbox, a German place-name, a Church of the Brethren. Afro-American communities also dot the landscape here and there on both sides of the ridge.

Loading peaches at the R.W. Handy Orchards, Woolwine, Virginia

7

Reece Billings
harvesting burley
tobacco, Alleghany
County, North
Carolina

As Franklin County gives way to Patrick County along the eastern slope, the piedmont valleys to the east seem to rise up closer to the Blue Ridge. By the town Meadows of Dan, the parkway straddles the plateau, and farms, pastures, and small communities lie on both sides. In the summer one sees hay, corn, and hazy blue fields of cabbage, as well as the wooden constructions of rural life: pasture fences, outbuildings, and weathered or white-painted houses and stores. Access roads to nearby communities connect to the parkway, which serves here as a local thoroughfare, and the traveler suddenly shares the road with pickup trucks and other such traffic.

Beyond Laurel Fork the Blue Ridge runs west and the parkway brings the traveler into Carroll County. The plateau remains to the right, but on the left the parkway overlooks the eastern slope that stretches down toward the piedmont town of Mount Airy. Off to the right a few miles is the thriving town of Galax, a factory center for furniture and other industry and the home of a famous annual fiddlers' convention. Beyond Galax lies the New River Valley.

As the parkway crosses into North Carolina, the landscape begins gradually to change. Alleghany County lies to the right, Surry County down the mountain to the left. The plateau landscape continues, studded with country Baptist churches, pastures, and plots of burley tobacco. But the parkway gradually plunges into a wooded terrain and is cut off from the nearby life. Logging joins farming as a means of livelihood, and the piedmont valley, with its farms and brightleaf tobacco plots, is more distant. Just past Cherry Lane, Surry County gives way to Wilkes on the precipitous, heavily wooded eastern slopes, and fences, churches, country roads, farm buildings, and clusters of houses are less frequent as the plateau falls away to a valley on the right. And beyond the community of Mulberry Gap, nature again seems to gain the upper hand.

Marvin Kimble and
Cassell Bowman
straining molasses,
Carroll County, Virginia

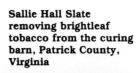

Sallie Hall Slate removing brightleaf tobacco from the curing barn, Patrick County, Virginia

Flume and wheel,
Walter Mitchell's mill,
Claudville, Virginia

Local and migrant
cabbage harvesters,
Goins brothers' farm,
Carroll County, Virginia

The Jarvis Farm

A family farm provides a close look at the Blue Ridge's cultural landscape. For Ernest Jarvis, on a walk around his farm in Alleghany County, North Carolina, memories and associations are as vivid as the farm's buildings, fields, and fences. The memories extend to the time of Ernest's grandfather Ira, who was born in the 1850s and worked the farm when it included 500 acres. The land was divided when Ira died in 1928, and Ernest's father, Kemper, the youngest son, inherited the thirty-odd acre tract with the house and outbuildings. Kemp, as he was known, bought some adjoining land and the farm now totals about 84 acres. When Ernest was a boy, seven or eight families lived along the mile of gravel road separating the farm from the highway, but now only one or two remain.

None of the family lives on the farm any more; Ernest and his wife and son live in a brick house on the main road. But his life and memories center on the farm. The family vegetable garden is where it has always been, and Ernest often visits and walks about the property.

His earliest recollection is of the time when he and a friend tried to steal a watermelon from the springhouse near the creek. The springhouse is also associated with memories of a more regular event: carrying water up the long hill to the house and carrying dairy products back down. The farm changed as Ernest grew up, and the biggest change was electrification:

> That spring took the place of the refrigerator till we got the lights in here. But I believe that milk and stuff tasted better when it run in the water than it did in the refrigerator. Yeah, we'd go down there and have buttermilk, and butter, and milk, in that spring. I know the water tastes better. When you go out of that bucket, just go there and bring it up out of that bucket from the spring, not run it through that pipe, it tastes a whole lot different, now, I can tell you that, it's better out of the spring.

Ernest cannot say why the buildings were so far from the water and strung out along the upper slope of the hill, but he said he thought the danger of flooding might have had something to do with it. The location of the buildings below the hill's crest does protect them from winter winds. And since they are all at about the same elevation, it's easy to get from one to the other.

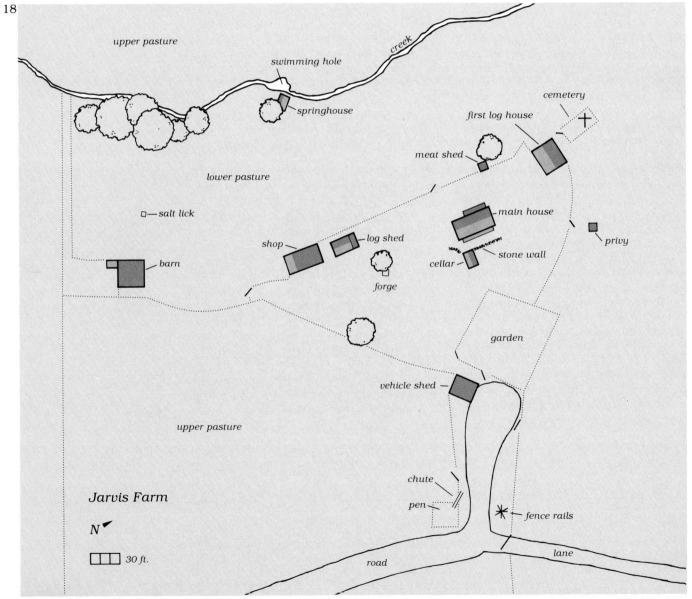

18

upper pasture

creek

swimming hole

springhouse

cemetery

first log house

meat shed

lower pasture

□—salt lick

shop

log shed

main house

barn

cellar

stone wall

privy

forge

garden

vehicle shed

upper pasture

chute

pen

✳—*fence rails*

Jarvis Farm

N ➤

▭▭▭ 30 ft.

road

lane

The farm plan comprises an inner area which was the site of the most frequent use, a ring of buildings that receive regular, year-round use, and a pair of seasonal buildings. The inner area runs from the privy and main house southward to the granary and shop, taking in the site of the old forge and, in spring and summer, the vegetable garden to the east.

The buildings that received year-round use when the farm was more active include the meat shed, the vehicle shed, and the springhouse. The seasonal buildings are the former dwelling at the north end of the complex and the flat-roofed barn at the south. They were filled with hay in summer and emptied to feed livestock in winter; the barn also sheltered cattle and horses in inclement weather.

Chestnut and locust trees from the farm provided the rails and posts for the fences that once sectioned it. About fifteen years ago, Ernest tore most of the fences out, replaced some with wire, and left only the section on the side of the hill above the house. Since he stopped growing corn and began using the land exclusively for pasture, less fencing was required. Rail fences were once economical because no cash was required. Today, forty or more years since a blight killed the chestnut trees, rails can be sold at a profit: "A hundred foot of rails will buy a spool of barbed wire," Ernest said, "and I believe it goes 1320 feet."

The following pages present a look at two of the farm's outbuildings and describe the five dwellings associated with the family.

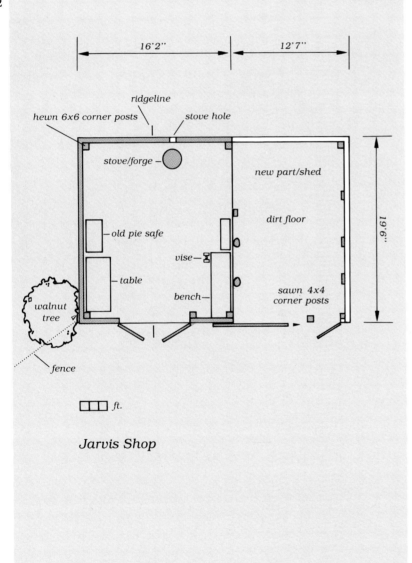

16'2"   12'7"

ridgeline

hewn 6x6 corner posts   stove hole

stove/forge —

new part/shed

old pie safe

vise—

dirt floor

19'6"

table

walnut
tree

bench—

sawn 4x4
corner posts

fence

☐☐☐ ft.

Jarvis Shop

Kemp Jarvis's Workshop. The floored blacksmith shop contains the tool benches and smithing equipment used by the Jarvis men over the years. The shop, built on the sharp slope of the hill, is supported by a drylaid foundation that offers storage space or shelter for animals underneath. The original part, with additional storage space above, employs large round logs with flat tops as floor joists and squarehewn vertical posts and vertical sawn boards for the walls. The shed addition was constructed entirely of sawn lumber at a later time to provide more workspace and storage for agricultural machinery. Some of the iron hardware on the shop was forged by the Jarvises.

Older Blue Ridge residents fondly remember a time when many goods were produced at home, but Ernest tempers his nostalgia with clear recollections of the work involved in hoeing corn, grinding sausage, and maintaining farm machinery. Of his father and grandfather, Ernest says, "They made everything; I don't reckon they bought anything, hardly." Tools and machinery were made and repaired in this workshop, connected by function to the blacksmith's forge which stood below a small tree nearby. The main work area, with its workbenches and vise, was on the ground floor; the loft was given over to the storage of lumber. The shed addition was used to store equipment.

B

A

The Jarvis Dwellings. The five houses associated with the Jarvis farm represent a cross-section of Blue Ridge homes from early settlement to the present. The three older houses are on the farm itself, and the two newer dwellings are on the main paved road about a mile away. The two log houses are the oldest, and although Ernest associates them with his grandfather they may have been built during the first decades of the nineteenth century, predating Ira by at least a generation.

The larger log house (A), probably once the farm's main dwelling, measures 26 by 20 feet. It was carefully constructed of hewn oak logs joined by half-dovetail corner-notching. The lower story once had a partition that divided it into a larger room with fireplace and stairs and a smaller room probably used for sleeping, a plan called "hall and parlor" by students of architectural history. The chimney and fireplace are gone, but the riven slats protecting the windows (B) remain. The building has been used to store wood and hay.

The smaller log house (C) is about 15 by 14 feet with a five-foot-wide corn crib added to the north wall. It is constructed of oak and chestnut logs with half-dovetail corner-notching (D), and its one-room plan is sometimes called "single-pen." There is no sign of a fireplace, nor could Ernest recall there ever having been one. He thought the house had provided extra lodging space for hired help or visitors. In Ernest's boyhood it served as a granary for buckwheat, rye, and oats. Both log structures are one and a half stories high.

D

F

Ernest said the frame house (E) was "close to a hundred years old," and it was the family home when he was growing up. It is a two-room, two-story house with a central chimney, one version of a plan often called "I house." Although the centrally located door and false front gable made for an impressive facade, the house does not have the central hallway often found in similar dwellings.

The living room was also the music room. Some evenings as many as six couples would dance there to the sounds of local musicians or records by the Carter Family, Roy Hall and the Blue Ridge Entertainers, and the Monroe Brothers. In the forties the front porch was refurbished, the back porch enclosed to make a kitchen, electricity installed, and the fireplaces closed. A wood-burning cookstove was added behind the central chimney, facing the new kitchen, and a wood-burning heating stove was installed (F).

Several factors influenced the family to vacate the house in the mid-sixties. Ernest got married and after about a year moved to a new brick house (G) on the main road. Kemp died, leaving his widow at home alone. And winter snows were a problem; a 1960 snowfall kept the family house-bound for ten days. When Ernest's mother moved to a mobile home next to his house, the farmstead was left unoccupied. She brought some furniture and several family pictures with her, and in 1978 Ernest was planning to sell many of the remaining house effects and farm tools.

E

G

"There's not eight hours on a farm."
Ernest Jarvis's autobiography begins with
stories of sunup to sundown work on the
family farm, and this story was passed
along to him by men who had worked with
his grandfather:

> Now, he really growed the grain. Now,
> I've heard this fellow say that he would
> get down, you know, on his knees and
> gather it up, you know, he was thresh-
> ing, you had to lay down sacks and
> stuff to keep that from spreading, you
> know, it'd—you'd lose it. And, he said,
> he said, "It's not what you made that
> done you good, it's what you saved."
> And they said they'd just sit there and
> you know that machine run, 'n' he
> would get up every little handful of
> that. He said that he told 'em that. And
> I've heard them fellows that run that
> machine say that. Well that's about
> right, though, it's not what you make,
> it's what you save.

Ernest attended school through the
seventh grade and when he was fourteen
began to work in his uncle's sawmill. Most
of his working life was spent in a sawmill
or cutting timber, at first with relatives
and after 1964 at a mill he owned and op-
erated himself. In 1969, his heart condi-
tion forced him to quit working. He often
visits the farm just to look around and
sometimes muses a bit on the subject of
work:

> But I really enjoy it. I enjoy working on
> a farm. I still do. Today I like to. And I
> like to sawmill, too, but I don't go
> around that sawmill cause it makes me
> sick when I go around there, you
> know, just to watch 'em, and 'cause I
> can't do it. Now I got attached to it,
> you get attached to them—to some-
> thing like that, just like you do your
> family about it.

Family attachments are strong for Ernest, and he said he plans to leave the
farm to his son Alan, born in 1971. He
would not consider selling the farm, he
said, because money could not buy him
happiness like this. "It makes me feel good,
now I'll just tell you that, just to come and
walk around on it. They has been people
wanted to buy this land; I told 'em, I said,
'It's not for sale.' "

Communities

**Town and Country
Barber Shop, Sparta,
North Carolina**

Patterns and Values

The population of the Blue Ridge is fairly dense and evenly spread throughout the countryside. There are incorporated towns, of course, but the sharp edge that separates the New England village from the surrounding farmland is seldom found here. The people of the region are bound together, nevertheless, by invisible networks of shared feelings and behavior. Their sense of community is reflected in stories like Ruth Holbrook's tale of how Traphill got its name.

> A drummer got drunk on pea liquor and the hotel, or the building where they kept boarders, they called it "hotel," was just across the road on top of the hill over here. And he started up to spend the night and he couldn't make it. And so they set a chicken coop over him, or a turkey trap it was. And he waked up, why he named it "Traphill." And they had a meeting then, the next night, and officially named it "Traphill."

A crossroads hamlet like Laurel Fork or Traphill is home for people with common backgrounds and shared values. Patterns that reflect these values are visible everywhere in the community—in the look of a store or restaurant, in the form of stories or seating arrangements at the barbershop or quilting bee, or in the types of music and movement at a dance. Dance is the

Quilting at the Baptist Church, Meadows of Dan, Virginia

very metaphor for community, both in the way dancers join in patterned expression and in the kaleidoscopic movement of dancers within the pattern.

The sets of couples on the dance floor reflect the groups within the community. Teenagers in an automobile and storekeepers on a sofa have their own circles and connections. The clientele at the barbershop and the quilters in a church basement are defined by gender and, to some degree, by age. Their shared values are symbolized by decoration: a "Flower Garden" quilt pattern, a chart showing game fish, a stuffed bobcat, and racing-type auto hood latches.

Beyond these complex networks of local community lie larger and less intimate communities of region and nation as well as narrower "communities of interest." The selection of a local woman as Miss America is greeted by a display of pride. At events like the Galax Fiddler's Convention—an annual extravaganza that attracts forty thousand visitors—the Blue Ridge both expresses itself as a part of the upper South and shares the nation's perception of it as a region.

The fox hunter's field trial brings together men from several states; their sport is akin to, yet distinct from the sort of fox hunting associated with horses, formal riding attire, and grand estates in Virginia. Here the pickup truck replaces the horse, and the attire is the usual local garb. But the fundamental cultural values are much the same, involving the domestic pleasures of raising the fox hounds; the social pleasures of leisure and conversation before, during, and after the hunt; the auditory pleasure of listening to and appraising the baying of the hounds; and the philosophical pleasure of contemplating the eternal pursuit of the eternally elusive fox.

Twin County Foxhunters
Club field trial,
Carroll County, Virginia

Clinton and Mae Iroler
in their store, Carroll
County, Virginia

Tex Drive In,
Stuart, Virginia

36

The Sparta Restaurant,
Sparta, North Carolina

**Shockley's Shell
Service Center,
Hillsville, Virginia**

Kyle Creed with local
and visiting musicians
at the Galax Fiddler's
Convention

Carroll County, Virginia

40

Fancy Gap Dance

For eight or nine years, the Friday night dance at Fancy Gap Elementary School has brought pleasure to local residents and provided revenue for its sponsors. Organized by the PTA, the event has raised thousands of dollars for the school and various groups within it. The dance helped pay for a class trip to Washington, D.C., a new dishwasher for the cafeteria, and a new fence for the basketball court.

On August 25, 1978, the dance benefited the local Cub Scout pack. About a hundred people attended, most from within fifteen miles of the school, but some from as far away as fifty miles. Visitors to the region also came, like the migrant farm laborers who helped bring in the cabbage crops. Music was supplied by the Peach Bottom String Band from nearby Independence. The caller was E. G. Branscome from Fancy Gap, who joined the dancers on the floor and called as he moved through the figures with them. Solo "flatfoot" dances and couple dances were intermixed with figure dances, but the dancers never formed the western square of four couples familiar to square dance clubs throughout the United States.

Some figure dances drew as many as forty couples onto the floor, but "Chase the Squirrel" was danced by about twenty-five. The band played the tune "Liberty." Like most of the figure dances performed in the region, the actual "Chase the Squirrel" movement is preceded and followed by opening and closing sections in which all the dancers join in larger figures. The opening section lasted about two minutes,

the "Chase the Squirrel" section about two and a half, and the intricate closing nearly six.

The opening consisted of a series of circular figures, first with all the dancers in one ring and then with an inner ring of women and an outer ring of men. The section was brought to a close by the call "Swing your partner and chase the squirrel."

At some dances in the region, the "Chase the Squirrel" figures are executed with calls to guide the dancers, but Branscome did not call this section at Fancy Gap. The dancers relied on the music and their own sense of time to change from one figure to the next, and several couples were out of synchronization with the rest at certain moments. The captions for the diagrams on pages 44–45 indicate some of the calls used for "Chase the Squirrel" at other dances in the area.

The "Chase the Squirrel" section was brought to a close with the call "Swing your partner and promenade." After the couples promenaded around the ring, Branscome led them up the center. As they reached the other side, the couples crossed, and gents peeled off to the right and ladies to the left, forming two adjacent, oval-shaped rings and meeting at the other end. The pattern was repeated with couples, then pairs of couples; finally, a massive row four couples wide moved up the center. This was followed by a meandering serpentine led by Branscome, and with his final "Swing your lady, thank the lady" the dance ended.

Chase the Squirrel

Gent (square)

Lady (circle)

The "nose" line indicates
the direction faced.

1. Each couple, hands
joined, finds and faces
another couple.

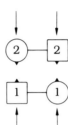

2. Led by the lady, the
first couple begins to
dance around the
second couple.

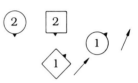

5. Led by the gent, the
first couple begins to
dance around the
second couple.

6. The first couple has
danced to a position
behind the second
couple.

9. All four join hands
and circle left.

10. In a figure
sometimes called "Swing
your opposite," each
gent swings the lady of
the other couple.

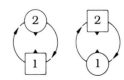

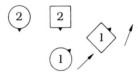

3. The first couple has danced to a position behind the second.

4. In a move sometimes called "Gents fall through," the first couple moves through the second couple.

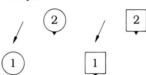

7. Lady falls through.

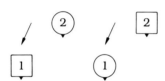

8. The couples return to their original positions.

11. In a figure sometimes called "Swing your own," the two original couples swing.

12. Each couple moves across the floor to meet another couple.

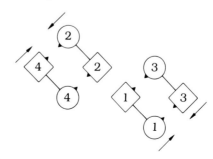

Religion

Laurel Glenn Regular
Baptist Church,
Alleghany County,
North Carolina

Churches

Sunday morning Service, Laurel Glenn church

There are churches in the Blue Ridge region in every community and at many a turn or rise in a country road. The buildings are mostly frame, painted white, and unadorned or modestly decorated. Like the region's religious life, they are modest, direct, and pervasive.

Eliza Davidson found that Alleghany County contained sixty-five churches representing eighteen religious groups (*see* "North Carolina Country Churches," in *Carolina Dwelling*, ed. Doug Swaim, Raleigh, 1978). Three-quarters of the churches are Baptist, but as Davidson notes, the autonomy of Baptist congregations and the absence of a church hierarchy has led to the development of several Baptist denominations in America. Although Southern Baptists form the largest Protestant denomination in both the United States and North Carolina, Southern Baptist churches in Alleghany County are outnumbered four to one by other Baptist denominations, including Primitive, Missionary, Regular, Freewill, and Union. The New Covenant Baptist Association in the region was founded by blacks after Emancipation. Other churches in the county include Methodist, Church of the Brethren, Presbyterian, various Gospel, Holiness, and Pentecostal groups, Jehovah's Witnesses, Latter Day Saints (Mormon), and Roman Catholic.

Singing after the service, Laurel Glenn church

For most Protestants the Sunday morning service is the central event in the week's calendar. Many congregations, however, add singing or prayer services Sunday, Wednesday, or Saturday evenings and often a weekly business meeting. In addition, many people listen to religious radio broadcasts on Sundays and at other times as well. This portion of the Blue Ridge is nationally famous for its string bands, in which fiddle and banjo play traditional dance tunes, but semiprofessional religious singing groups are at least as numerous and are often heard on the radio or at special church services.

If, despite this rich weekly fare, the spirit flags, the yearly calendar offers the revival—a week or two of nightly meetings, sometimes combined with radio broadcasts. Many churches hold an annual revival in the church building or in a tent outside. Other revivals are conducted by itinerant preachers, who may erect a tent in a vacant lot or at the edge of town.

Annual church homecomings reunite a congregation with members who have moved away. Periodic communion services may attract distant members as well as friends who belong to other churches in the area. Baptist association meetings in the summer collect the congregations of a dozen or more member churches. At all such events group spirit and unity is reinforced by enthusiastic hymn-singing and the social "dinner on the ground," a meal on the church grounds or in the fellowship hall where members share local cooking and baking.

Immersion baptism is not the exclusive rite of Baptists but is practiced by some other denominations as well. Some churches have built special indoor pools, but most preachers and congregations prefer a suitable creek or stream. Here the union of soul and Savior is conducted in a setting that also unites man and nature.

Baptism, Big Reed
Island Creek, Carroll
County, Virginia

**Dinner on the ground,
New Covenant Baptist
Association annual meeting,
Grayson County,
Virginia**

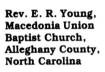

Rev. E. R. Young,
Macedonia Union
Baptist Church,
Alleghany County,
North Carolina

58 **Rev. Coy Combs and
Mrs. Ruth York,
Sunday morning,
WHHV radio, Hillsville,
Virginia**

**Skyline Independent
Baptist Church, Carroll
County, Virginia**

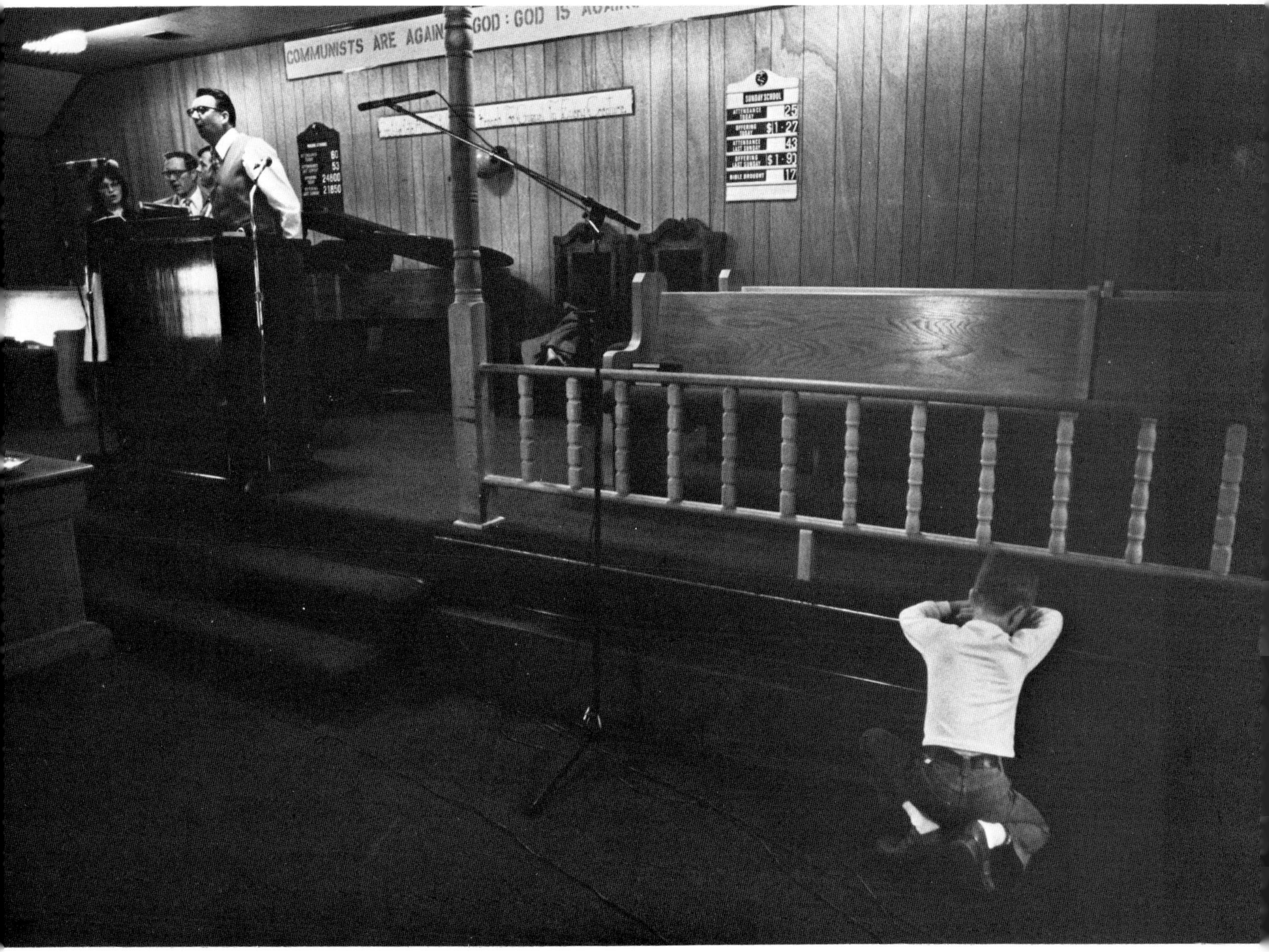

**Receiving the spirit,
Rev. Robert Akers's
tent service,
Galax, Virginia**

**Rev. Robert Akers's
tent service,
Galax, Virginia**

Galax Primitive Baptist
church, Galax, Virginia

Footwashing

In many of the rural communities in the area represented by this book, Primitive Baptist churches and their congregations are from the stable, mature core of the community. Baptists have been in the region since at least the very early nineteenth century and when, between about 1820 and 1840, the conservative Primitive Baptist denomination began to develop, it flourished in the southern mountains. Primitive Baptists believe in predestination and salvation by grace and neither evangelize nor conduct Sunday school classes. The Church and its services are egalitarian; ministers do not receive a salary, congregational singing is preferred to solo or small group performances which would spotlight individual talent, and great deference is paid to each member's opinions. This democratic spirit is heard in the remarks offered by Elder Horace E. Walker at the annual communion service conducted at the Galax Primitive Baptist Church in Galax, Virginia, August 13, 1978. The excerpt below was part of a lesson on the meaning of footwashing extemporized by Elder Walker, who had traveled from Roanoke to help conduct the service:

> I fully, wholeheartedly believe that foot-washing is part of the communion service. I'm just not satisfied without it. And I desire to talk to your benefit and learning, a little bit about it. . . .
>
> When He had ended the Passover of the Jewish, Mosaic Law, He done a new thing, He took bread and brake it and gave thanks and said, "Take, eat." And

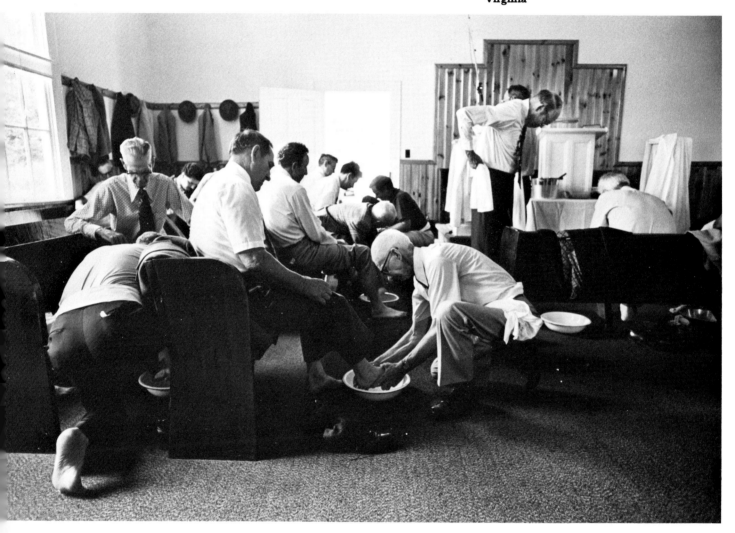

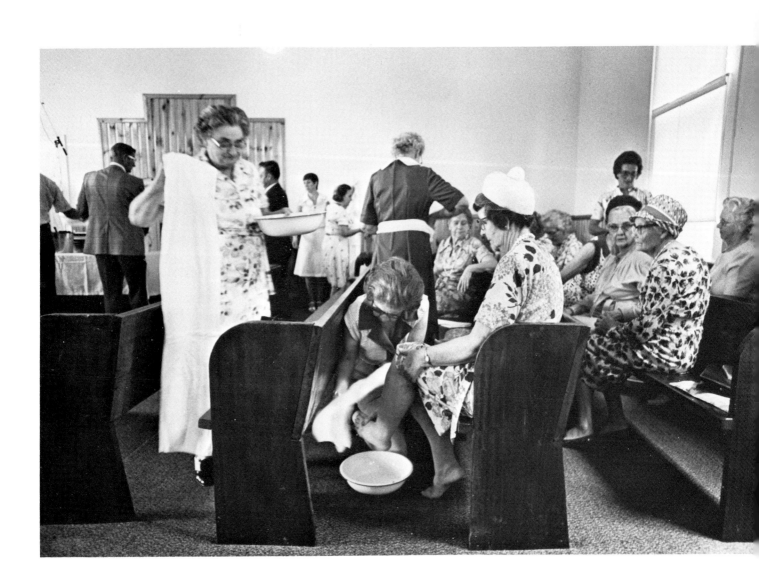

likewise He took the cup. And when He had finished this, He rose from the table and began to wash the disciples' feet. The only place you'll find it in the New Testament—it's not in Matthew, it's not in Mark, it's not in Luke, but it is in that gospel of John, the recording of the washing of the disciples' feet. Some say it's not that important because it wasn't included with the other disciples. But everything that our Lord and Master did was for a purpose. . . .

Jesus came into a Pharisee's home one time and this Pharisee was strict according to the letter of the law of Moses. And while He was in this Pharisee's home, Jesus was in his place of abode, a Samaritan woman came into his presence and this Pharisee says in his mind and heart, says "If he was a prophet, he would know what kind of a woman she is that stands before him. She's a sinner. Maybe the worst kind of sinner. She's not fit to stand in His presence." And then this woman began to anoint His head with oil and and wash His feet with her tears. And He turns to Simon the Pharisee and He says, "Simon, seest thou this woman?" Well, Simon has possibly 20–20 vision, she was standing right at his presence, he couldn't help but see the woman. But that isn't what our Lord meant. He said, "Simon, seest thou this woman? Thou has not anointed my head with oil nor washed my feet since I entered thy house. But this woman has not ceased since I entered thy house to wash my feet and anoint my head with oil." Then He turns to that woman and says, "Thy sins are forgiven." Now that woman is a figure of the church, the bride, the people of God.

So He takes a basin and pours a little water in it and begins to wash the feet of the disciples. Do you not see the symbol in the bread and the wine? Why isn't the feet a symbol? Lord, keep my feet in the paths of righteousness. Direct my feet because—it is of my feet that I stand or fall. The lowly feet. Oh yes, you can say it means humbleness, sincerity, forgiveness, repentance on the part of a fellow believer one to another. But He also says something else. There's a cleansing effect of water. We are baptized in the river of water, and we also drink from that fountain of the tree of life, water and Jesus. . . .

I believe in footwashing. I believe it's a part of the communion service. I do not believe it ends as Paul says, "As often as ye take this cup and eat this bread, you do show the Lord's death till He come." I believe that those disciples that was in that upper room, when they had the bread and the wine served to them, that he washed their feet, I believe footwashing was included as the New Testament rites of the church ordinances. I believe it's just as much a part of the church's obligation and duty to do this as it is the bread and the wine. But I wouldn't want to draw swords and knives against my fellow brethren that would say, "No, this is not part of the ordinances of the church." But personally to me it is, and Jesus says, "If ye know these things and do them, happy are ye that do them."

So, brethren, we have poured the water in the basin—and that basin is a symbol and it means something, and that water in that basin means something, and the water that is washing the feet means something. And the towel that he girded Himself with, to wipe them clean and dry, may signify the glories of putting on immortality, the righteousness of Christ. It means a lot of deep things to me. But nevertheless, we hold no bars or ill will with anybody that don't see it like I do. But I want to do it, because it means something personally to me.

So, when He had poured the water into the basin, He girded Himself with the towel, He removed His outer garmets. Not His inner garments, as some might accuse Him. But His cloak, His outer "overcoat," you might say. And He took a towel then and girded it round His waist and He begins to wash the disciples' feet. Let us, brethren, wash one another's feet.

Communion service, Galax Primitive Baptist Church, Galax, Virginia

Carrie Severt

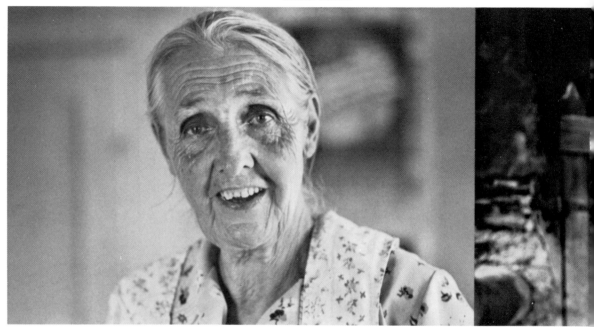

Portraits

McKinley Brim   **D. J. and Janet Keith**

Carrie Severt

Edd and Carrie Severt raise cattle on the Alleghany County farm they have rented for the last seventeen years. They like their one-hundred-year-old house, including the hand-dressed lumber in the ceiling. That ceiling can be a problem, though; the resin seeping from the wood ruins every coat of paint they try to put on it. Carrie uses the cellar beneath the front room to store forty bushels of potatoes and home-canned food.

Like so many Blue Ridge families, the Severts produce most of the food they consume. They raise a large garden, planting when they can according to the signs in Blum's Almanac. Carrie cans more than three hundred quarts of fruits, vegetables, and meat each year. One year this included eighty quarts of beans and sixty quarts of peaches, as well as cracklings, carrots, grape juice, mustard pickles, peach preserves, ribs, beef stock, tomato juice, and chow-chow. She makes apple butter in three different ways, and every so often she and her daughter make it the old-fashioned way in a black pot in the back yard. She prefers that method, for the apple butter just seems to taste better. Carrie also pickles beans, kraut, and corn on the cob. The children eat the pickled corn as a snack: "the young-uns come down here, and get it out of the can," she says. The Severts frequently raise and butcher their own hogs. Carrie fries and cans more than seventy pints of sausage a year, and they cure the rest of the pork, which will last them for the entire year.

If a husband pulls one way and the wife another, you'd just as well to go, 'cause they both got to work together if you make a good marriage of it.

Canning carrots

Pan biscuits

Carrie is an excellent cook, and a noontime meal generally includes both biscuits and cornbread made from scratch. Other regional favorites that might be on the Severt table include fried chicken or chicken and dumplings or chicken pie, pork tenderloin, corn, green beans, cole slaw, tomatoes, and several kinds of pickles. Like many area cooks, Carrie prepares her meals on a woodburning stove. Most women own both electric and wood stoves; the one they use depends upon the season and the food they are preparing.

"You name it, and I've done it," Edd Severt says. He has worked at general farming, dairying, and sawmilling at a water-driven sawmill built by his grandfather and run by his father. He built houses, and, in 1937, worked on the Blue Ridge Parkway pouring concrete headwalls and building retaining walls. He used to take his children up to the parkway to show them the structures he helped build. Today Edd farms from a pickup truck; arthritis and a new steel hip prevent him from using his tractor.

Both Edd and Carrie were raised in Ashe County. They walked long distances to the old Boggs schoolhouse, usually going barefoot until Thanksgiving "when Daddy sold his turkeys." But they had fun too; the boys "played tricks" and, during the winter, went sledding on homemade sleds with locust runners. "We was crackerjacks then," he chuckles. The girls often played catch with a ball made out of yarn unraveled

Grandson James Edwards joins Edd for lunch

Edd Severt on the farm

Sharing the afternoon mail

from socks. They built playhouses out in the woods where they constructed miniature doll beds from moss. Sometimes they even decorated their own houses with long strings of popcorn.

"We had rough living back then," Edd observes, and both Severts remember the New River flood of 1916. Carrie's father had just returned from the mill with freshly ground sacks of flour when the river started rising. The family had to flee, and when they returned, Carrie remembers peering through a window and seeing all that flour floating in the muddy water inside the house. Edd almost lost his grandfather in that flood. The old man returned home in a boat to retrieve a valuable trunk; as he paddled out of the house the swirling water caught the boat and was about to engulf it when the craft suddenly lodged against a partially submerged springhouse. To this day, that building is called the "springhouse that saved my grandpa's life."

The Severts recently celebrated their golden wedding anniversary with a special reception in Sparta. They were childhood sweethearts in grade school. "We was always crazy over one another," Carrie says. After their schooling ended in the seventh grade, they went their separate ways, but later met again at a funeral in the community. He walked her home, and they have been together ever since. Married by a magistrate at her home in 1928, they raised five children, all of whom live in the state. They confess to having their "little spats"

now and then, but they still try "to pull together." They were raised on a farm, Carrie
says, and they knew what they were getting
into when they got married. "We've worked
together all our lives; I help him, and he
helps me."

Carrie's favorite pastime is quilting.
"I'd just as soon quilt as to eat," she says,
adding for emphasis, "and I ain't kidding."
She begins quilting after Christmas and
continues until the gardening season begins in April. One winter she and her
daughter pieced forty quilt tops, including
some of her favorite patterns: the Wheel,
the Lone Star, and the Tree. While her
daughter pieces the quilts on a sewing machine, Carrie prefers to sew hers "by the
finger." Scraps that family and friends are
happy to give her are snipped and stitched
to form the quilt tops. She uses blankets
from the Chatham Blanket Factory for the
filler, and once her daughter sewed together tiny tobacco sacks to make a quilt
lining. Most of the excess quilt tops she
shares with the needy or with her family.
Each of her eight grandchildren has received one of her quilts.

Carrie quilts on a winter evening after
the outside chores are finished. She cannot
watch television while she quilts because
the work itself demands too much concen-
tration. She hangs her homemade quilting
frames from the bedroom ceiling and works
in that room. Carrie likes to quilt in the
fan pattern because, she believes, "it shows
up prettier," but Edd has to "lay off" the
semicircular lines for her with a crayon.

**Quilting in the
fan pattern**

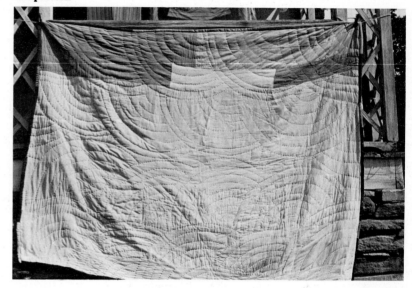

**Carrie milks
one-handed**

"I'll make out to him that I can't lay them off; he can do it easier than I can." She uses quilts on all the beds in her house and washes most of them in the washing machine. She will dry-clean the special quilts, but likes to air all of them. "Airing does them more good than washing them," she says. Edd sometimes gets angry with Carrie, saying she would let him starve so she could keep on quilting. She laughs in assent but adds, "I never let him go hungry."

Except for the twelve years she spent cooking at a local school, Carrie's entire life has been spent on a farm. "There ain't been nothing outside nor in that I haven't done," she says, but adds, "There ain't much I like to do in the house." She tends to the cooking, washing, churning, and milking herself, and since she broke her wrist last winter, she has become a one-handed milker. She works side by side with Edd cutting wood in summer, and in winter it takes both of them nearly a whole day to feed silage and hay to their sixty or seventy cattle.

Removing suckers—the plant's extra shoots—from brightleaf tobacco

McKinley Brim

*If a man quit work, I believe he'd
get just no 'count for nothing. . . .
If you retire and not have nothing to
do, you'll soon die off, get sick and
die off.*

McKinley Brim is in his early eighties and
works a bit slower than he did a few years
ago, but retirement is far from his mind.
Like other brightleaf tobacco farmers in the
land below the ridge, McKinley's workday
in late summer is long and hard. The tobacco must be "primed," or picked, proc-
essed in the flue-curing barn, and brought
to the auction to be sold. Priming consists
of picking the best two or three leaves on
the plant. In the six weeks or so when
brightleaf ripens, several passes are made
through the field, priming progressively
higher and higher up the stalk. McKinley
transports the freshly picked leaves to the
barn on a "priming slide," a wooden sled
that slides easily across the hilly soil. In
1978 he had planted his rows so close together that the "driveways" were too nar-
row for a tractor and the slide was pulled
by McKinley's mule.

The farm lies between the Dan and Ar-
arat Rivers in Patrick County, Virginia. It
is in a rural neighborhood known as "the
Meadowfields community" or "the Clarks
Creek community," home for black families
since slavery. According to McKinley's
neighbor, Jesse Hatcher, four family names
predominate in the community's history:
Carter, Smith, Brim, and Hatcher. Sorting
out family connections can be hard, however, because in the years before Emancipation, changes of ownership often meant
changes in surname, and written records
from the nineteenth century are rare.

Birdie Brim

Like many men in the Blue Ridge, McKinley spent part of his life working for wages in southern West Virginia. Most of the men worked in the mines, and their savings helped buy land and start families. But the dark tunnels scared McKinley, and he worked above ground on the railroad. He went to West Virginia for a short time as a teenager and just laughs when asked if he managed to save up some money. He came back and got married when he was eighteen, he said, and had to borrow to get started.

Birdie Carter was sixteen when she and McKinley were married, and five boys and two girls of the couple's ten children are still living—some in the neighborhood and some in places like Mt. Airy, North Carolina. Doris lives at home with her parents, and Fred, who is director of secondary education at the county high school, lives next door.

**Kitchen scraps
for the chickens**

Fred Brim

The church at Clarks Creek was founded in 1892, and the first services were held under a white oak tree where the building stands today. According to eighty-eight-year-old Deacon Jesse Hatcher, one of the senior members and a close student of the church's history, the congregation was Primitive Baptist until just after the turn of the century. But the church wanted to depart from some of the more conservative practices, and they joined other black churches in the new Progressive Primitive Baptist denomination. Deacon Hatcher says the church started a Sunday school in 1907 and toward the end of the twenties added an organ and piano to accompany congregational singing.

The first building was log, followed by a frame and then a brick structure which was struck by lightning and burned down just a few years ago. In 1978 the members were hard at work erecting a new building. While the sanctuary was being completed, services were held in the basement.

McKinley Brim joined the church relatively late in life, after he had reached his sixties. Birdie has been a member for many years, and the children are active in the church. Fred directs the choir, and both he and Doris play the piano. Many residents of the Blue Ridge tell how their religious conversion resulted from an intense personal experience, but McKinley simply says he reached his own conclusion. "I just decided to myself," he explained, "a man has to leave this world some of these days and if he left unprepared, why he'd just be lost, according to the Bible."

Clarks Creek
Progressive Primitive
Baptist Church

The choir: Doris Brim
at right; Fred Brim
at the piano

**The new
flue-curing barn**

McKinley has two tobacco barns, an old one made of chestnut and the new barn shown here. It was built about ten years ago in a traditional form using traditional materials and techniques. Little cash was required since the structure was made from local oak and black gum logs and built by McKinley's friends and neighbors. "I just asked a bunch of hands in," he said, "and had a working."

The barn is sixteen feet square and wooden tier poles divide the interior into four-foot "rooms." The tobacco leaves are tied to sticks four and a half feet long which are hung across the tier poles. Brightleaf tobacco is cured by hot air forced through a system of flues in the bottom of the barn. The air is heated by burners or fireboxes: McKinley burns local oak and locust wood to save the cost of fuel oil. The best cure is achieved if the heat is applied steadily for as long as three days, and McKinley used to sleep at the barn at night to keep the fires burning. His concession to age is that he now goes back home to sleep:

> Of course I quit that staying at night. I go to bed. [laughter] I used to cure down here and, and fix me a bed, a little house, and got in under and laid down, and the next morning the fire had gone out. Had to come and get the lamp oil to get it started. So I just quit staying at night and just fire it in the day.

McKinley checks the
curing fires at
his tobacco barn

McKinley has been a farmer for the last half-century or so, first on land owned by a white man and then for the last several years on his own fifty-odd acres. The workday begins at five when McKinley feeds his livestock. The chore of feeding poultry later in the day falls to Birdie, who shares with Doris the task of cooking the meals.

McKinley's affection for his livestock often animates his conversation, as when he tells how he used molasses to sweeten feed or explains that he shears the mane and tail of his mule so it will look good. He recalls with pleasure a 1,400-pound workhorse he had, "as fat and round as a butterball," that could pull a big number 13 plow as well as two ordinary horses. And when his picture was taken with an old milk cow, he joked that she did not give milk any more but that he could not bear to part with her.

Morning coffee

**Birdie and McKinley
Brim at home**

Janet and D.J. Keith

Janet and David Joel Keith teach at Floyd County High School, near Floyd, Virginia. D.J. teaches mathematics and is the faculty sponsor of the Math Club. Janet teaches English and some elective courses offered by the English Department, including one for freshmen which looks at the region's traditions. Janet is an avid and sympathetic student of local history, and her knowledge and insight make her an ideal choice to teach the course. As in the Georgia high school where students have written the articles collected in the *Foxfire* books, Janet is partly motivated by the need to find congenial topics for student essays. She explained that when students write about the tales and reminiscences they have collected, they learn about the region's traditions as well as how to improve their writing:

> A couple of the boys did some really nice things like going to an old log house on their property and trying to recreate it in scale form using little sticks. And a lot of the kids have come back to me later saying, "You know, as a result of what we talked about in class I have some of my grandmother's or great-grandmother's old letters," and they'll come and show them to me. Or say, "I sat down the other Sunday with my grandmother and did like you said—go through the old pictures and put tape on the back and write who it was while she could still tell me."

Not every aspect of culture is suitable for a public forum, and a relative of Janet's

94

was dismayed to hear that a lecture on folklore revealed the text of a spoken charm used to stop bleeding. The use of this charm is a family tradition, Janet explained, and successfully cured D.J. when he had recurring nosebleeds. But its effectiveness depends upon private teaching and use. If she were to discuss the charm in her class, she would not reveal certain elements of it:

> I might say something to the effect that, "Well, this was something that a number of people still strongly believe in, which used to be passed from man to woman." And I would probably not say which verse, although it might be there in a book for them. It's the kind of thing, you know, where you're touching on your own—whether you call them superstitions or whether you call them beliefs or whatever they may be. I think the fact that I grew up in this country gives me a bit more of a touch for what to include or what not to include in that kind of a discussion.

Foxfire and the spirit of the Bicentennial have inspired the academic study of local traditions in school, but there are also traditions connected with school life itself. Students congregate and talk at the end of the lunch hour in the designated smoking block near a doorway, or cruise through town in the evening, following a route nearly as well designated as the smoking area. And "Spirit Week," preceding the homecoming football game, is a school tradition sanctioned by the administration.

**Floyd County
High School**

Floyd County's three high schools were consolidated in 1962, when Janet and D.J. were juniors. They returned as teachers in 1971, and Janet recollects that two or three years later the cheerleaders and student council expanded the homecoming pep rally into a week of activities. "For eighth graders coming up," she said, "it's a tradition to continue." Each day has a prescribed dress, including "tacky," "pioneer," and "fifties," the last inspired more by current television programs than by the actual fashions of that decade.

School rules are relaxed for Spirit Week. Some students show off by bringing empty whiskey bottles, and, as Janet puts it, "They wear getups they can get away with on that day and couldn't get away with any other time."

Let the spirit move you on the 1st day of the week. Today is THE day all clean people put on their Tackiest clothes cause Monday is Tacky Day.

David Keith

The Keiths farm over four hundred acres and maintain a herd of nearly one hundred beef cattle. In addition to teaching and farming, D. J. used to coach football and baseball. But coaching took time that he preferred to spend with his family and paid a supplement of only "about a quarter an hour," so he decided to give it up. The Keiths' acreage is in three or four locations and the work of farming it keeps the whole family occupied.

Preparations for winter include cutting and baling hay, harvesting grain, and storing silage. After the harvest the cornstalks are ground, transported, and shaped into a "bunker silo" which is then covered by a plastic sheet. Janet says the whole job is "one of the hardest day's work you can imagine," in a tone of voice that recalls her husband's characterization of the people of the region. "They're hard workers," D.J. said, "but they don't take on the work as drudgery; they take on the work as pride."

**Janet packs
down the silage**

Janet Keith's thirty-second birthday cake was a gift from her mother, baked to order by the high school's home economics class. The whole family turned out for the celebration: the Keiths' children, David, Jennifer, and Kevin, and both Janet's and D.J.'s parents. Janet's parents, Ruth and Freeman Slusher, live nearby, while Weeda and Dewey Keith live next door at the bottom of the hill. D.J. was raised in his father's house and his father had been raised across the road in the old family home, no longer used as a dwelling.

During the evening, David slipped up and surprised his mother by smearing butter on her nose. The custom is well-known in the region, and Janet said it even happened with some frequency at the high school:

> The kids do it in the lunchroom. Every once in a while you'll hear a "Happy Birthday" burst out and someone will have found—whether it's butter or something similar—to smear on noses. And of course the element of surprise is supposed to be there.

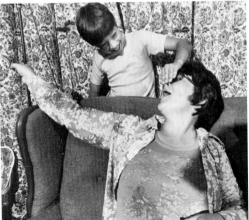

David butters his mother's nose.

Jennifer, Kevin, and Janet

Freeman Slusher, Janet's father, is a member of the Korn Kutters, a string band with the tight ensemble sound for which the region is famous. His guitar and Willard Clower's banjo provide the rhythmic counterpoint that supports the melodic lead of Ivan Weddle's fiddle and George Slusher's harmonica. The group plays for various dances and functions with a repertory of dance tunes ranging from "Bill Cheatham" to the less well-known "Long Tongued Woman." When asked for the words to this tune one evening at a family gathering, the wife of one of the players cheerfully supplied this bit of lyric: "She can talk a man to death before he gets his breath," and the group dissolved into laughter.

The picture on the left takes us into the family's past; it portrays the Weddle brothers and sister of three generations ago. Harvey, who died before the picture was made, is represented by a portrait. Joel, in the lower right corner, is D.J.'s great-grandfather and the source of his middle name. The Weddles were members of the German Baptist Brethren, a denomination nicknamed "Dunkards" and now called the Church of the Brethren. Brethren congregations are still active in the region, although the plain dress of the Weddles' day has been modified. Janet, a Baptist, said she once attended a funeral and was surprised to see some men without neckties, until she learned they were members of the Brethren who believed neckties were an unnecessary adornment.

The Korn Kutters

The Keiths' family backgrounds are a mixture of English and German and thus mirror the region's settlement patterns. The Keiths came to America from England in the eighteenth century at about the same time that the Schlossers, now anglicized as Slusher, immigrated from Germany to southeastern Pennsylvania. Before the end of the eighteenth century Christoper Schlosser migrated down the Shenandoah Valley, reportedly heading for North Carolina. Janet and D.J. have retraced the family's route, admired the fine farmland along the way, and wondered why the Slushers selected hilly Floyd County as their new home. Land may have been available there, of course, but family stories tell of short rations and bad weather that brought the trip to a premature halt. "Maybe it *was* that rather than their getting here and saying, 'Oh what a beautiful place,' " Janet wistfully concedes. "I'd like to think," she adds, "that they came here and said, 'Oh what a beautiful valley, let's just stay.' "

Sources and Resources

Overview

**Lemley Slate with
Rhody and Kate,
Patrick County,
Virginia**

Several excellent texts and bibliographies present an overview of the Southern Mountain region, including the Blue Ridge. Although dated, Campbell's *The Southern Highlander and His Homeland* and Kephart's *Our Southern Highlanders* contain valuable information. Ross's bibliography includes a helpful filmography compiled by Robert J. Higgs. Three periodicals which frequently treat aspects of Blue Ridge folklife are the quarterly *Appalachian Journal,* published by Appalachian State University, Boone, North Carolina, the quarterly *Blue Ridge Institute Newsletter,* published by the Blue Ridge Institute, Ferrum College, Ferrum, Virginia, and the annual *Folklore and Folklife in Virginia,* published by the Virginia Folklore Society, University of Virginia, Charlottesville.

Appalachian Bibliography.
> Morgantown: West Virginia University Library, 1970. Second edition, 1972. Third edition, 1975.

Campbell, John C.
> *The Southern Highlander and His Homeland.* New York: Russell Sage Foundation, 1921.

Kephart, Horace.
> *Our Southern Highlanders.* New York: The Macmillan Co., 1913. Reprint edition, New York: The Macmillan Co., 1967.

Ross, Charlotte, *editor.*
> *Bibliography of Southern Appalachia.* Boone: Appalachian Consortium Press, 1976.

Special Topics

County histories are often useful sources of information and lore; the two cited here are especially helpful. *Fisher's River Scenes and Characters* contains local color and boyhood memories from the pen of Harden Taliaferro (pronounced "Tolliver"), a nineteenth-century Baptist minister from Surry County, North Carolina. Jones's "Studying Mountain Religion" treats the region's religious expression in general, while Sutton's article and Sexton's book look more closely at particular groups. *The Chalice and the Covenant* is the history of an association of black Baptist churches in the central Blue Ridge. The region's traditional architecture, crafts, and other aspects of material culture are the subjects of the works by Swaim, Wilhelm, and Eaton. Footnotes in *Carolina Dwelling* will guide readers to additional works.

Eaton, Allen H.
  Handicrafts of the Southern Highlands. New York: Russell Sage Foundation, 1937. Reprint edition, New York: Dover Publications Inc., 1973.

Fields, Bettye-Lou, *editor.*
  Grayson County: A History in Words and Pictures. Independence, Virginia: Grayson County Historical Society, 1976.

History of Alleghany County 1859 through 1976: Sparta, North Carolina.
  Winston-Salem: Printed by the Hunter Publishing Co., [1976?].

Jones, Loyal.
  "Studying Mountain Religion." In *A Guide to Appalachian Studies,* special edition of *Appalachian Journal,* volume 5, number 1, Autumn 1977, pp. 125–30.

Sexton, Mark S.
  The Chalice and the Covenant: A History of the New Covenant Baptist Association 1868–1975. Winston-Salem: Hunter Publishing Co., 1976.

Sutton, Brett.
  "In the Good Old Way: Primitive Baptist Traditions." In *Long Journey Home: Folklife in the South.* Special issue of *Southern Exposure,* volume 5, number 2–3, Summer-Fall 1977, pp. 97–105.

Swaim, Doug, *editor.*
  Carolina Dwelling: Towards Preservation of Place: In Celebration of the North Carolina Vernacular Landscape. (The Student Publication of the School of Design, volume 26). Raleigh: North Carolina State University, 1978.

Taliaferro, Harden E.
  Fisher's River Scenes and Characters. New York: Harper & Brothers, 1859. Reprint edition, New York: Arno, 1977.

Wilhelm, Eugene J., Jr.
  "Folk Settlements in the Blue Ridge Mountains." *Appalachian Journal,* volume 5, number 2, Winter 1978, pp. 204–45.

Music

There are many record albums of the string band music for which the Blue Ridge is famous and some which present the region's folksong, spoken word, and religious music traditions. This list is a sample of currently available records. An important survey of Primitive Baptist hymnody, edited and annotated by Brett Sutton, is now in preparation by the University of North Carolina Press. Most of the following can be bought from the publishers or from mail order outlets like Andy's Front Hall (R.D. 1, Wormer Road, Voorheesville, New York 12186), County Sales (Box 191, Floyd, Virginia 24091), or Roundup Records (Box 474, Somerville, Massachusetts 02144).

Biograph RC 6002. *Fields and Wade Ward*. Songs and instrumental music. (16 River Street, Chatham, New York 12037).

Blue Ridge Institute 001. *Virginia Traditions: Non-Blues Secular Black Music.* Various artists. Notes by Kip Lornell. (Ferrum College, Ferrum, Virginia 24088).

Blue Ridge Institute 002. *Virginia Traditions: Ballads from British Tradition.* Various artists. Notes by Blanton Owen.

County 505. *Charlie Poole and the North Carolina Ramblers: Old Time Songs Recorded from 1925–1930.* Songs and instrumental music. (Box 191, Floyd, Virginia 24091).

County 510. *The Red Fox Chasers.* Reissue of songs and instrumental music recorded from 1928–30.

County 533–5. *Round the Heart of Old Galax: Traditional Music of Grayson and Carroll Counties, Virginia.* A three-volume series with various artists, including Ernest V. Stoneman and Wade and Fields Ward.

County 701. *Clawhammer Banjo.* Various artists, including Wade Ward, Kyle Creed, and Fred Cockerham.

County 702. *Larry Richardson and Red Barker and the Blue Ridge Boys.* Songs and instrumental music in the bluegrass style.

County 723. *Back Home in the Blue Ridge: Fred Cockerham, Tommy Jarrell, and Oscar Jenkins.* Songs and instrumental music. Notes by Richard Nevins.

Folk-Legacy 1. *Frank Profitt.* Songs and banjo music. Notes by Sandy Paton. (Sharon Mountain Road, Sharon, Connecticut 06069).

Folk-Legacy 14. *Ray Hicks.* Jack tales. Notes by Cratis Williams, Lee B. Haggerty, and Sandy Paton.

Folkways 3811. *Traditional Music from Grayson and Carroll Counties [Virginia].* Various artists. Songs and instrumental music. (43 West 61st Street, New York, New York 10023).

Heritage 15. *The Walker Family: Family Circle.* Unaccompanied religious singing. (Rt. 3, Box 278, Galax, Virginia 24333).

Heritage 22. *Eight Miles Apart: The Shelor Family and the Kimble Family.* Songs and instrumental music.

Library of Congress AFS L–47–48. *Jack Tales: Told by Mrs. Maud Long of Hot Springs, North Carolina.* Two volumes. (Motion Picture, Broadcasting and Recorded Sound Division, Library of Congress, Washington, D.C. 20540).

Library of Congress AFC L–69–70. *Children of the Heav'nly King: Religious Expression in the Central Blue Ridge.* Various artists; material recorded as part of the Blue Ridge Parkway Folklife Project. Notes by Charles K. Wolfe. Forthcoming.

Mountain 302. *June Apple: Tommy Jarrell, Kyle Creed, Audine Lineberry, and Bobby Patterson.* Instrumental music. (Rt. 3, Box 278, Galax, Virginia 24333).

Rounder 0026. *E.C. Ball with Orna Ball and the Friendly Gospel Singers.* Songs and instrumental music. (186 Willow Avenue, Somerville, Massachusetts 02144).

Rounder 0057–8. *Old Originals: Old-Time Instrumental Music Recently Recorded in North Carolina and Virginia.* A two-volume series. Notes by Tom Carter and Blanton Owen.

String 802. *Emmett W. Lundy: Fiddle Tunes from Grayson County, Virginia.* Instrumental music recorded in Galax, Virginia, for the Library of Congress, 1941. Notes by Tom Carter. (22 Upper Tollington Park, London N4 3EL, England).

Sovereign Grace 6057–6058. *Old Hymns Lined and Led by Elder Walter Evans: Sparta, North Carolina.* Primitive Baptist congregational hymn singing. (The Baptist Bible Hour, P.O. Box 17037, Cincinnati, Ohio 45217).

Archives and collections

**Drying beans,
Alleghany County,
Virginia**

Much of the richness of Blue Ridge culture has been collected but not published. The archives listed here contain significant holdings from the region and serve as centers of research and scholarship.

Appalachian Collection
Belk Library
Appalachian State University
Boone, North Carolina 28607
Sound recordings, photographs, and over ten thousand bound volumes.

Archive of Folk Song
American Folklife Center
Library of Congress
Washington, D.C. 20540
Established in the Library in 1928, the archive has extensive collections of Appalachian material. The materials from the Blue Ridge Parkway Folklife Project are part of the Library's collections.

Archives of Appalachia
Sherrod Library
East Tennessee State University
Johnson City, Tennessee 37601
Historical papers, family collections, the collected videotapes produced by Broadside Television, and other materials.

Bascom Lamar Lunsford Collection
Appalachian Room, Memorial Library
Mars Hill College
Mars Hill, North Carolina 28754
Materials amassed by one of the region's pioneer collectors.

Blue Ridge Institute
Ferrum College
Ferrum, Virginia 24088
The institute oversees a wide variety of projects to preserve the traditional culture of the region: the Blue Ridge Folklife Festival is held each fall; the Blue Ridge Farm Museum features reconstructed farms from three settlement periods; and the Blue Ridge Heritage Library is an archive of folklore research materials.

Joseph S. Hall Great Smoky Mountains Collection of Speech, Music, and Folklore
1455 Lemoyne Street
Los Angeles, California 90026
Hall has collected in the Smokies since 1937, including accounts of early times, traditional farming practices, foodways, and folktales. Much of his collection has been duplicated by the Archive of Folk Song in the Library of Congress.

North Carolina Archive of Folk Lore and Music
Hill Hall
University of North Carolina
Chapel Hill, North Carolina 27514
Field recordings and other materials, primarily from the state. Much of this collection has been shared with the Archive of Folk Song in the Library of Congress.

University of Virginia Folklore Archive
Virginia Folklore Society Archive
WPA Folklore Archive
University of Virginia
Charlottesville, Virginia 22904
The University of Virginia Folklore Archive holds the Arthur Kyle Davis Collection of sound recordings and manuscripts, an index to the Virginia Folklore Society Archive, and an extensive collection of recent field recordings. The Virginia Folklore Society Archive and the WPA Folklore Archive are in the university's library.

Credits

Blue Ridge Harvest is based on fieldwork conducted during the Blue Ridge Parkway Folklife Project. Members of the project team wrote the texts for the various sections: "The Region," by Alan Jabbour; "The Jarvis Farm," by Carl Fleischhauer, based on fieldwork by Thomas A. Adler and Howard W. Marshall assisted by Richard MacCamant and George Price; "Patterns and Values," by Alan Jabbour; "Fancy Gap Dance," by Carl Fleischhauer and Margaret Owen; "Churches," by Carl Fleischhauer; "Carrie Severt," by Geraldine N. Johnson; "McKinley Brim," by Carl Fleischhauer, based on fieldwork by Patrick Mullen assisted by Harley Jolley and Wes Leishman; and "Janet and D. J. Keith," by Carl Fleischhauer, based on fieldwork by Thomas A. Adler, Carl Fleischhauer, and Terry and Lyntha Eiler. Quotations in the text have been transcribed from sound recordings created by the project. Some have been edited for readability.

Blue Ridge Harvest was designed by William Rawley of the Division of Typography and Design at the Government Printing Office.

The following list identifies the photographers and provides the negative numbers for the photographs in this book. All of these pictures, or copies of pictures in the case of historic photographs, are part of the collection at the Library of Congress created by the Blue Ridge Parkway Folklife Project. The photographers are Thomas A. Adler, Lyntha Scott Eiler, Terry Eiler, Carl Fleischhauer, Geraldine N. Johnson, Howard W. Marshall, Patrick B. Mullen, Blanton Owen, Margaret Owen, and Charles K. Wolfe.

Cover: Lyntha Eiler BR8–3–20543/29
Title page: Carl Fleischhauer
    BR8–5–20189/26
Contents: Lyntha Eiler BR8–5–20543/12A
iv: Lyntha Eiler BR8–4–20263/10A
3. Terry Eiler BR8–6–20423/2A
4–5. Lyntha Eiler BR8–18–20346/20A
6. Lyntha Eiler BR8–LE64–2 (original in color)
7. Lyntha Eiler BR8–6–20223/27
10. Lyntha Eiler BR8–2–20493/29A
12. Terry Eiler BR8–13–20542/30
13. Carl Fleischhauer BR8–16–20302/26
14. Terry Eiler BR8–11–20345/19
15. Terry Eiler BR8–2–20202/19A
16. Lyntha Eiler BR8–6–20414/4

18. Drawing based on fieldwork by Thomas A. Adler
19. Top: Geraldine N. Johnson BR8–3–20257/6A
19. Bottom: Lyntha Eiler BR8–14–20421/18
20. Top: Thomas Adler BR8–1–20398/34
20. Bottom: Lyntha Eiler BR8–5–20414/6A
21. Drawing based on fieldwork by Thomas A. Adler
22. Drawing based on fieldwork by Howard W. Marshall
23. Top: Howard W. Marshall BR8–HM4–6 (original in color)
23. Bottom: Geraldine Johnson BR8–3–20257/10A
24. Top: Lyntha Eiler BR8–16–20421/4
24. Bottom: Lyntha Eiler BR8–5–20414/33A
25. Top: Lyntha Eiler BR8–14–20421/20
25. Bottom: Lyntha Eiler BR8–10–20414/24
26. Lyntha Eiler BR8–6–20421/13A
27. Top: Lyntha Eiler BR8–5–20414/16A
27. Bottom: Geraldine N. Johnson BR8–12–20443/36
29. Lyntha Eiler BR8–5–20421/14A
30–31. Geraldine N. Johnson BR8–3–20170/20A
32. Lyntha Eiler BR8–6–20263/8A
33. Lyntha Eiler BR8–4–20421/37
35. Terry Eiler BR8–9–20344/15A
36. Terry Eiler BR8–7–20423/12
37. Carl Fleischhauer BR8–13–20229/6
38. Terry Eiler BR8–9–20203/28A
39. Thomas A. Adler BR8–38–20544/14A
40. Lyntha Eiler BR8–3–20777/5
41. Terry Eiler BR8–3–20203/13
42. Terry Eiler BR8–TE26–15 (original in color)
44–5. Chart based on fieldwork by Margaret Owen
46. Blanton Owen BR8–3–20343/22 (Garden Creek Baptist Church, Wilkes County, N.C.); BR8–33–20544/7A (negative reversed; Laurel Glenn Regular Baptist Church, Alleghany County, N.C.); BR8–3–20343/29 (Garden Creek Church)
47. Blanton Owen BR8–7–20229/33 (Pine View Primitive Baptist Church, Carroll County, Va.); BR8–33–20544/3 (Garden Creek Baptist Church); BR8–7–20229/32 (Pine View Primitive Baptist Church)
48. Lyntha Eiler BR8–5–20190/29
49. Terry Eiler BR8–2–20231/5
50. Terry Eiler BR8–8–20423/35A
51. Lyntha Eiler BR8–6–20493/11
52. Lyntha Eiler BR8–15–20346/26
53. Terry Eiler BR8–3–20423/27
54–5. Blanton Owen BR8–7–20229/34
56. Geraldine N. Johnson BR8–6–20424/19
57. Terry Eiler BR8–2–20777/9
58. Charles K. Wolfe BR8–3–20485/24A
59. Terry Eiler BR8–8–20542/33
60. Terry Eiler BR8–3–20232/28A
61. Terry Eiler BR8–4–20232/4A
62–3. Lyntha Eiler BR8–1–20171/30A
64. Lyntha Eiler BR8–5–20231/19A
65. Lyntha Eiler BR8–5–20231/14A
67. Lyntha Eiler BR8–6–20171/22

Carson Creek, Surry
County, North Carolina

**Canned goods, Patrick
County Fair, Stuart,
Virginia**

**Back cover: Lowe
home, Lowgap,
North Carolina**

FOR SALE BY THE SUPERINTENDENT OF DOCUMENTS
U.S. GOVERNMENT PRINTING OFFICE, WASHINGTON, D.C. 20402

☆ U.S. GOVERNMENT PRINTING OFFICE : 1984 O - 433-476 : QL 2